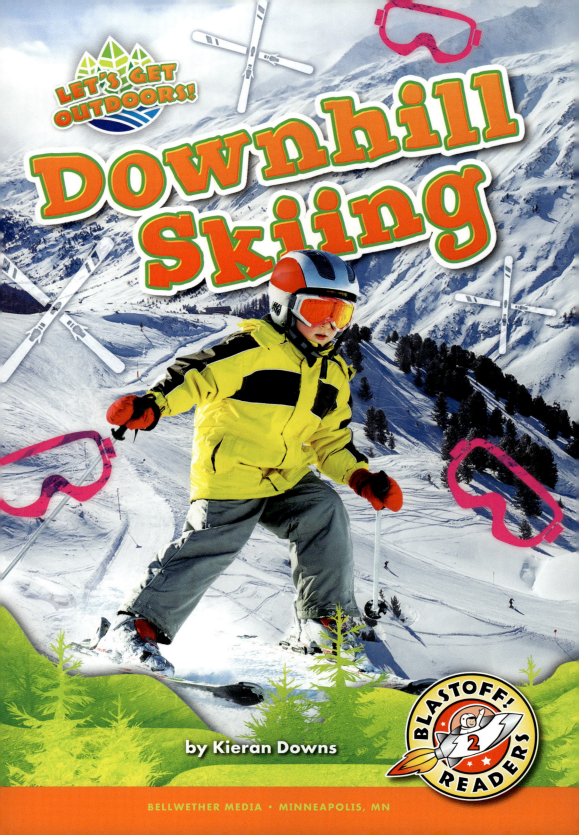

Blastoff! Readers are carefully developed by literacy experts to build reading stamina and move students toward fluency by combining standards-based content with developmentally appropriate text.

LEVELS

Level 1 provides the most support through repetition of high-frequency words, light text, predictable sentence patterns, and strong visual support.

Level 2 offers early readers a bit more challenge through varied sentences, increased text load, and text-supportive special features.

Level 3 advances early-fluent readers toward fluency through increased text load, less reliance on photos, advancing concepts, longer sentences, and more complex special features.

★ **Blastoff! Universe**

Reading Level

Grade K

Grades 1–3

Grade 4

This edition first published in 2024 by Bellwether Media, Inc.

No part of this publication may be reproduced in whole or in part without written permission of the publisher. For information regarding permission, write to Bellwether Media, Inc., Attention: Permissions Department, 6012 Blue Circle Drive, Minnetonka, MN 55343.

Library of Congress Cataloging-in-Publication Data

Names: Downs, Kieran, author.
Title: Downhill skiing / by Kieran Downs.
Description: Minneapolis, MN : Bellwether Media, 2024. | Series: Blastoff! readers. Let's get outdoors! | Includes bibliographical references and index. | Audience: Ages 5-8 | Audience: Grades 2-3 | Summary: "Relevant images match informative text in this introduction to downhill skiing. Intended for students in kindergarten through third grade"– Provided by publisher.
Identifiers: LCCN 2023035144 (print) | LCCN 2023035145 (ebook) | ISBN 9798886877991 (library binding) | ISBN 9798886878936 (ebook)
Subjects: LCSH: Downhill skiing–Juvenile literature.
Classification: LCC GV854.315 .D678 2024 (print) | LCC GV854.315 (ebook) | DDC 796.93–dc23/eng/20230807
LC record available at https://lccn.loc.gov/2023035144
LC ebook record available at https://lccn.loc.gov/2023035145

Text copyright © 2024 by Bellwether Media, Inc. BLASTOFF! READERS and associated logos are trademarks and/or registered trademarks of Bellwether Media, Inc.

Editor: Elizabeth Neuenfeldt   Series Design: Andrea Schneider   Book Designer: Josh Brink

Printed in the United States of America, North Mankato, MN.

Table of Contents

What Is Downhill Skiing?	4
On the Hill	8
Downhill Skiing Gear	14
Downhill Skiing Safety	18
Glossary	22
To Learn More	23
Index	24

What Is Downhill Skiing?

Downhill skiing is a winter sport. It is also called alpine skiing. Skiers go down hills.

Some skiers race.
Most people ski for fun!

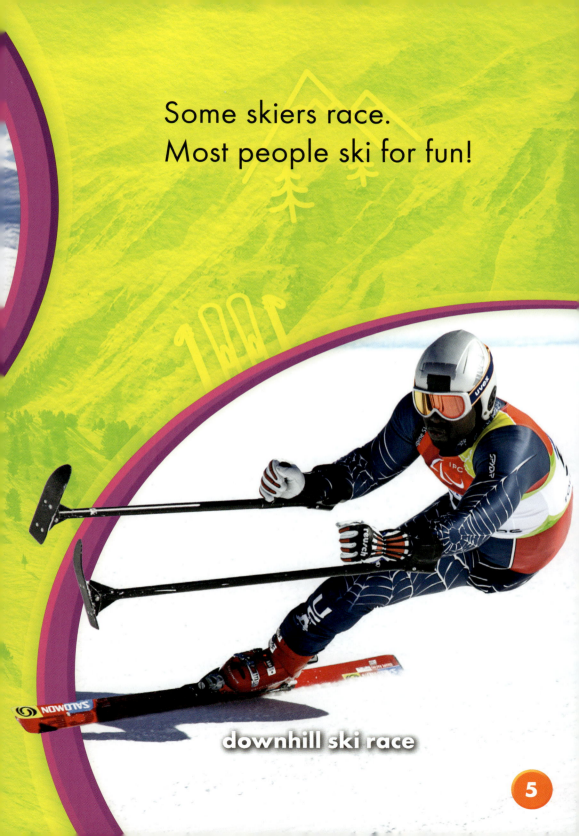

downhill ski race

People all around the world downhill ski. Most people downhill ski at **resorts**.

Favorite Downhill Skiing Spot

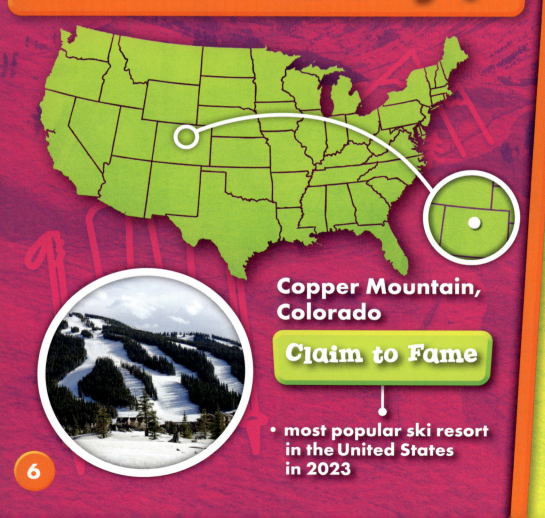

Copper Mountain, Colorado

Claim to Fame

- most popular ski resort in the United States in 2023

Resorts **groom** trails for skiers. Trails are often called **runs**.

On the Hill

Skiers often ride **chairlifts** up hills.

To ski downhill, skiers push off their poles. This gets them moving. They make turns as they ski.

← chairlift

New skiers learn to ski on **bunny hills**.

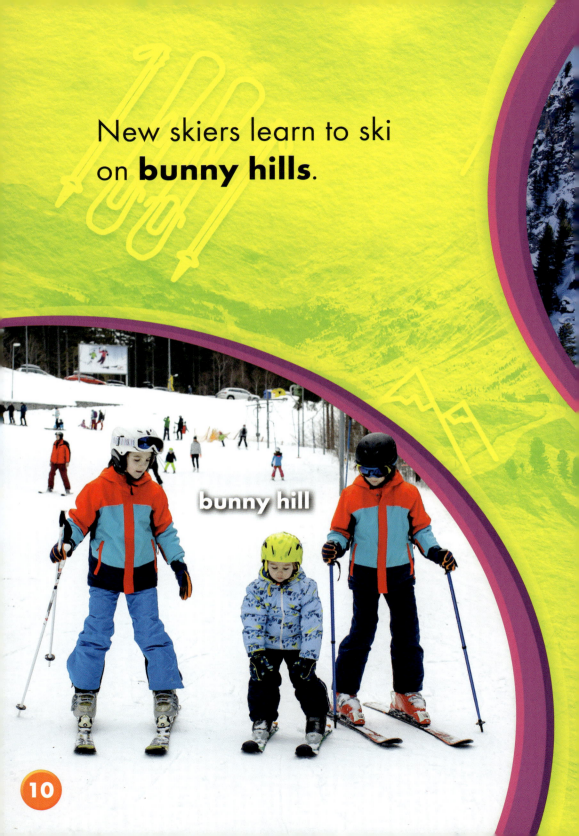

bunny hill

When skiers are ready, they move to bigger hills. Bigger hills have different ski runs.

levels sign

Ski runs have different **levels**. Green circles are the easiest. Blue squares are **intermediate**.

Black diamonds are for **advanced** skiers. **Double** black diamonds are for **experts** only.

Ski Run Levels

easy

intermediate

advanced

experts only

Downhill Skiing Gear

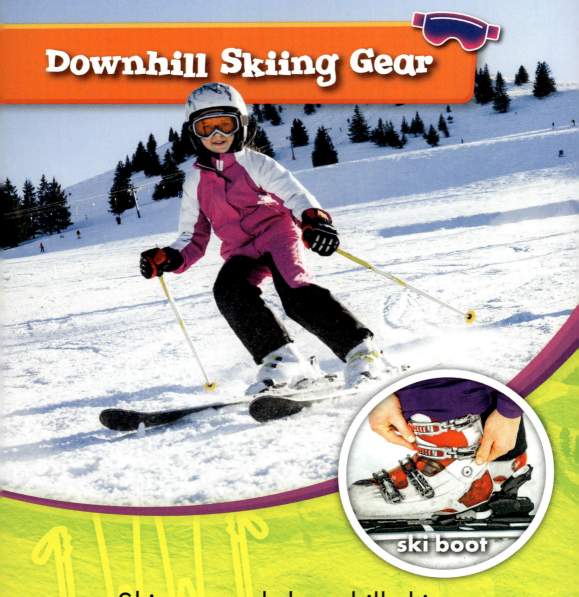

ski boot

Skiers need downhill skis. Special boots keep skiers connected to their skis.

14

Poles help skiers steer and **balance**.

Downhill Skiing Gear
- helmet
- goggles
- skis
- poles
- boots

Skiers must stay warm! They wear jackets, snow pants, and gloves.

Helmets keep skiers' heads safe. Goggles cover their eyes.

helmet
goggles

Downhill Skiing Safety

ski lessons

Skiers make sure they have the right gear. They must always wear helmets.

Skiers can take lessons. They should know how to use chairlifts.

Skiers should ski with others. They choose runs that match their level.

Skiers must follow the rules for ski runs. Staying safe keeps skiing fun for everyone!

Glossary

advanced—having a lot of skill

balance—to stay steady and not fall

bunny hills—gentle hills where beginners learn to ski

chairlifts—chairs attached to cables that skiers ride to reach hilltops

double—having two of something

experts—people who have a lot of knowledge or skill in a certain area

groom—to make trails neat and ready for skiing

intermediate—having some difficulty

levels—ways of telling how hard ski runs are

resorts—ski areas that people visit to ski and rest

runs—courses or trails

To Learn More

AT THE LIBRARY

Gish, Ashley. *Alpine Skiing*. Mankato, Minn.: Creative Education, 2022.

Leaf, Christina. *Cross-country Skiing*. Minneapolis, Minn.: Bellwether Media, 2024.

Sabelko, Rebecca. *Mountains*. Minneapolis, Minn.: Bellwether Media, 2022.

ON THE WEB

Factsurfer.com gives you a safe, fun way to find more information.

1. Go to www.factsurfer.com.
2. Enter "downhill skiing" into the search box and click 🔍.
3. Select your book cover to see a list of related content.

Index

alpine skiing, 4
boots, 14
bunny hills, 10
chairlifts, 8, 19
favorite spot, 6
gear, 15, 18
gloves, 16
goggles, 16
groom, 7
helmets, 16, 18
hills, 4, 8, 10, 11
jackets, 16
lessons, 18, 19
levels, 12, 13, 20
poles, 8, 9, 15

race, 5
resorts, 6, 7
rules, 21
runs, 7, 11, 12, 13, 20, 21
safety, 18, 19, 20, 21
skiers, 4, 5, 7, 8, 10, 11, 13, 14, 15, 16, 18, 19, 20, 21
skis, 14
snow pants, 16
trails, 7
winter, 4

The images in this book are reproduced through the courtesy of: ER_09, front cover (hero); Tatiana Popova, front cover (background); Rocksweeper, p. 3 (skis); Sergey Novikov, pp. 4, 16-17; George Blonsky/ Alamy, p. 5; chapin31, p. 6; Cybernesco, p. 7 (ski resort); SharpLumberjack, p. 7 (run); gorillaimages, p. 8; imagean, pp. 8-9; tatyana_tomsickova, p. 10; Nahlik, p. 11; Imgorthand, p. 12; jweller, p. 12 (levels sign); Lumi Images/ Alamy, pp. 14-15; Niko_Cingaryuk, p. 14 (ski boot); FamVeld, p. 15; VisualCommunications, p. 16; Blue Jean Images/ Alamy, pp. 18, 20; Altrendo Images, p. 19; Paul Biris/ Getty Images, p. 21; Petr Bonek, p. 23.